CW01486550

Several of these beautiful poem
of a man's separation from his
are painful to read, but so r
eternal hope that only Chris
passion and sensitivity in every poem as John Hermon
seeks to understand God's overwhelming love for him
and mankind.
Fiona Castle, author and public speaker

John Hermon is not afraid to look at the wound of loss in
his own heart, and in that raw process find healing.
These are psalms of lament, in touch with both the
human and divine. I would give this book to anyone who
has been bereaved – poetry often opens doors into our
being that other forms of writing can't.
*Shaun Lambert, Senior Minister of Stanmore Baptist Church
and author of* A Book of Sparks

Honest, personal, compelling, moving, memorable and
well written – John's words resonate as we travel with
him through emotional and spiritual turmoil following
the death of his beloved wife, to end in a place of
deepened faith, real hope, and new life.
Chris Leonard, author and writing facilitator

Sometimes

I

Write

Words

John Hermon

instant
apostle

First published in Great Britain in 2013

Instant Apostle
The Hub
3-5 Rickmansworth Road
Watford
Herts
WD18 OGX

British Library Cataloguing-in-Publication Data

A catalogue record for this book is available from the British Library

This book and all other Instant Apostle books are available from Instant
Apostle:

Website: www.instantapostle.com
E-mail: info@instantapostle.com

ISBN 978-1-909728-02-8

Printed in Great Britain

Instant Apostle is a new way of getting ideas flowing, between followers of Jesus, and between those who would like to know more about His Kingdom.

It's not just about books and it's not about a one-way information flow. It's about building a community where ideas are exchanged. Ideas will be expressed at an appropriate length. Some will take the form of books. But in many cases ideas can be expressed more briefly than in a book. Short books, or pamphlets, will be an important part of what we provide. As with pamphlets of old, these are likely to be opinionated, and produced quickly so that the community can discuss them.

Well-known authors are welcome, but we also welcome new writers. We are looking for prophetic voices, authentic and original ideas, produced at any length; quick and relevant, insightful and opinionated. And as the name implies, these will be released very quickly, either as Kindle books or printed texts or both.

Join the community. Get reading, get writing and get discussing!

Sometimes I write words

Lord, sometimes I write words.

Sometimes I write words for You,

words which may please You,

words which may draw others closer to You,

words which may let Your Spirit flow into other lives.

Lord, I offer You these words,

and, Lord, I pray that You who live

    above,

       below,

          around

            and far beyond

the poverty of my words

may use them for Your glory.

Dedicated to Mandy

Who chose to share her life with me.

She fostered my dreams and forgave my failings,

she prayed with me and prayed for me,

she gave herself in joy and bore me my children,

she danced me to the end of love.

Now she is gone, what shall we say?

Let this be recorded:

She

laughed,

lived

and loved

all to the full,

and broke the mould of dull convention

following Jesus.

That is sufficient;

her record here is closed,

but now has begun

a song without end.

Contents

Foreword

I found reading this collection of poems to be a deeply moving experience. In them John touches the depth of his soul and connects with the wide range of feelings within. Having connected with them, he is able to find the profound and meaningful words to be able to convey his inner world.

These poems give voice to the journey of a pilgrim following the loss from this life of a precious partner and soul friend. John does not shrink from expressing the opposites of his feelings. In many of the poems, the reader can hear the deep cry of the heart calling out to God amidst the confusion of so many conflicting feelings.

Throughout the journey, John's faith shines through. Embraced within the feelings is a deep trust in the One who is his God. The poems convey the truth that it is possible to be truthful concerning feelings of anguish whilst continuing to trust in and experience the presence of God.

Dr Nigel Copsey, Tutor, Pastoral Ministry, Spurgeon's College

The womb of the dawn

This is the womb of the dawn,

and in this place of deep and fertile night

primeval living word was first outspoke:

'Let there be light!'

And all creation at that voice awoke.

This is the womb of the dawn,

and here is fusion of the Spirit's might

and love unbounded in the Word revealed.

'I am the Light!'

All darkness vanquished to that light shall yield.

The benefit of windows

Perhaps You, Lord, are the maker of windows.

Once, Lord, there was a wall between You and me – a wall of my making, not Yours – but You have pierced that wall and made a window for Your light to come to me in my darkness.

Sometimes, Lord, this is scary. I like to pretend to others that I am better, more gifted, more spiritual than I really am – but Your window gives You free access to every corner of my life; the parts which I like and which I think might please You, but also those which I prefer to keep hidden from gaze. All is now open to Your light, uncompromising and pure – and this makes me flinch.

But I thank You, Lord, that You do not use the window in my soul to seek out failings and condemn. Thank You that my window is open to You so that Your grace, Your forgiveness and Your love may freely enter. There need be no darkness now, but only the purity of Your light and the power of Your Spirit to guide my way.

I thank You, Lord, that Your window is open for me also. I look out from the narrow time-bound confines of my earthly life and I glimpse – just glimpse – something of Your beauty, Your love and Your faithfulness.

I like to think, Lord, that little by little You are making our window higher, deeper, wider, to allow more of Your light to come to me and to let me see and understand more of You.

And one day, Lord, the wall will be torn down and everything will become the window of Your grace. And You will call me out and up from the cramped limits of my life on earth to experience the full reality of Your presence. No more a glimpse through a window but life lived to the full – LIFE with YOU.

We pray:

'Lighten our darkness, we beseech thee O Lord ...'[1]

And we search for His light which shines in the darkness — for us!

Jesus said:

'I am the light of the world. Whoever follows me will never walk in darkness, but will have the light of life.'[2]

'In Him was life ...'[3]

---

[1] *Book of Common Prayer*, 1662.
[2] John 8:12.
[3] John 1:4.

No, this is wrong!

Written after my beautiful, brave and beloved wife went to be with her Lord, 5th June 2007.

No, this is wrong, I cried; this should not happen.

No, this is wrong – you should not lie so quiet,

so peaceful, pale and lifeless on your pillow

while dawn and sunlight chase away the night.

No, this is wrong, I cried; this should not happen.

No, this is wrong – you should not die and leave.

Stay with me now – let this not be the moment

for separation, loneliness and grief.

No, live; for in this favoured summer morning

you'll hear the birdsong, watch the flowers unfurl,

and see each grass blade lift its perfect jewel,

a diadem of dew, a flawless pearl.

And you and I should go and run together

and share the pulse and thrill of life reborn,

and joyful go to worship our Creator

who gifts us with the promise of this morn.

I cry in vain – for in this June-bright morning,

the Crab,[4] the Crab, the bloody Crab whose claw

has seized and squeezed her life achieves his purpose,

destroys her flesh; her heart will beat no more.

But Crab, you do not win – for at that moment

when finally you seem to win your prize

of life brought low to death – it's then she triumphs

and breaks your grip of pain and dread disease.

For she is gone to that eternal morning

where dawn and dew and worship never fade.

She runs unwearied with her Lord who called her,

a joyful, perfect, all-forgiven child.

---

[4] 'Crab' here, and in 'Cursed be the Crab' on page 22, is a reference to cancer.

Though I still have my favoured summer mornings

and hear the birdsong, watch the flowers unfold,

though love of God and friends and kin surround me,

I know that I must walk the road alone.

Alone I walk, but only for a season;

alone, but still a purpose to fulfil.

I live, and love, and cherish truth and beauty;

my treasure and my hope in Christ alone.

Cursed be the Crab

Cursed be the Crab.

The shadow of his bloody claw

outstretched to harm

still casts his winter shroud upon our lives

who wait and dream of all that might have been.

Today there is no happy birthday joy;

we do not laugh

and blow the candles on the cake,

recalling memories of a year of grace,

and read the greetings sent by friends and kin

to mark the day.

So shall I weep

and shout my anger to the heedless sky?

Not so, for in my heart secure contained

lies faith of steel that will not flinch nor turn

until the victory; the endless futile round

of life and death is broke; the promises

of purpose and of life eternal stand

secure in God.

Doomed is the Crab!

His power will fade, for God has set a day

when righteousness and health and peace and joy

and perfect justice evermore shall reign.

Doomed is the Crab, for in that final day

his carapace is shattered and his claw,

at last destroyed and impotent for harm,

consumed for ever in the lake of fire.

Lord Jesus, come!

Written 3rd December 2010 for Mandy's 70th birthday

Remember me!

You never asked me to remember you.

Perhaps you knew

the probing blade of loneliness

in times of beauty solitary unshared

and empty-bedded wakefulness

would keep your memory living in my soul.

Perhaps you knew.

Our rainbow days

These are our April jewelled rainbow days
of sun and shadow, cloud and shafting rain.
The full-hued beauty of the light to us revealed,
refracted in the teardrops of our pain.

Where is peace?

Peaceful dappled sky.

Content, yet still in grief, I

go to lie alone.

Impasse

Will time truly heal?

Lest memories fade I cherish

the pain of my wound.

Loss lines

Tonight, Lord, I am angry and sad – again.

I have heard of a life quenched,

a marriage destroyed,

a family deprived,

a husband facing life alone.

More tears, more suffering, more pain.

Lord, have we not suffered enough?

Tonight, Lord, I have to admit,

Job is way ahead of me in his faith and devotion to You.

Tonight, Lord, with all my heart I can bless Your name

for the riches You give through those who hold me close,

for Your Word and Spirit present in my life,

for Your promises, Your Love and Faithfulness,

for Your beauty revealed each day to ear and eye,

for Jesus.

But, Lord, I find it hard to bless You

for what You have taken away.

Yes, I have precious memories of the life entwined with mine,

a living hope, a destiny secure,

but the dark pall of loneliness still clouds my skies,

and my bed is empty.

Lord, I say it again –

Yours is the Kingdom

Yours is the Power

Yours alone is the Glory – for ever and ever, Amen!

But tonight, Lord, Your Bride is sad,

desolate and waiting Your coming.

O Lord, how long?

Where is Your Dawn?

How long until

there is no mourning, death, crying or pain?

Lord, I cry to You,

I long for You!

Come, Lord Jesus!

So much...

So much depends on you,

for if the flame of love be quenched

the dark awaits me

and the night shall be

my closest friend.

Transformation

A moment – one, just one – is all it takes.

Her heart not beating and her breath not drawn,

so I, bereft, am

instantly

no longer her husband.

Breaking the circles

The circles of the minutes and the hours,

the circles of the days and of the weeks,

the circles of the seasons and the years

contained within the circle of my life,

birth, growth, maturity, decline and death,

confine and hem me in; can I escape?

An ancient teacher said that all is vain

and has no meaning; save the endless round

of what has always been since time began.

But no!

Escape from the encircling circumstance

of life was hers, and now is mine to grasp.

Like stones flung skyward from the circled sling,

we both shall find, beyond the bounds of time,

a pure perfection far beyond our ken,

and destiny attained through love alone.

When can I go?

After the shroud

The power of His breath
rips the clouds asunder.
Where once was dreary misery,
conceived in shades of grey,
the sun shines through and colours flare
at His command.

The power of His death
and resurrection
rips the shroud asunder.
Where once was dreary hopelessness,
conceived in shades of grey,
the Spirit's beacon flame ignites
at His command.

When the dark cloud
of death, despair and stalking fear
is torn away,
what colour will He paint your life?

Before the storm

Before the storm
you were my lamp; when time's no more,
the last grain counted through the narrow glass,
your flame shall burn again.

Before the silence
you were my psalm; when time's no more,
the tyranny of age and death undone,
in harmony not heard since earth began
your song shall rise again.

Written 3rd December 2009, Mandy's 69th birthday

God said

LET THERE BE LIGHT!

'The light shines in the darkness, and the darkness has not overcome it.' (John 1:5)

Faith is not

knowing clever answers

to difficult questions

but knowing

that the Answer exists.

You are beyond

O God, my God,

You hide Yourself in light.

You are the One beyond my understanding,

You are the One beyond my wildest dreams,

You are the One beyond the poet's words.

Lord, how can I worship You in spirit and in truth?

Lord, I give You my words –

    untainted by dissembling or pretence,

    I pray that they may be

    conceived in purity.

    And when there is no music in my soul

    accept as praise the yearning of my heart.

Lord, how can I worship You in spirit and in truth?

Lord, I give You my acts –

    though they be stumbling, partial, incomplete,

    I pray that they may be

    the earnest of my plea

    to see Your Kingdom come, Your will be done,

    the servanthood You choose to enact through me.

Lord, how can I worship You in spirit and in truth?

Lord, I give You myself,

I give You my love,

I give You my life,

nothing held back.

Advent

Lord Jesus, when You came,

You came

    for the poor

    and the despised.

Lord Jesus, when You came,

You came

    for the rich

    and for the kings.

Lord Jesus, when You came,

You came

    for the busy

    and for those who slept,

    knowing nothing.

Lord Jesus, when You came,

You came

for all.

So let me see again –

You came for me.

Power

God said, 'My power

is perfected in weakness', so

He was born a child.

Soundscape of Bethlehem

A woman moans.

A baby gasps for His first breath

and cries for her breast.

A song of peace and prayer

drifts in the night

in Bethlehem,

for God has come

and the world is changed!

Christmas is for me –
and it's personal!

If choirs of angels sang the song of peace

    on earth for all,

    it was for me,

    that I might know

the peace of God which is His gift to me.

If Jesus, God's own Son, became a babe,

    helpless and poor,

    it was for me,

    that I might know

that He forsook His throne for love of me.

If God could choose to set aside His power

    to share our world,

    it was for me,

    that I might know

when I am weak His Spirit strengthens me.

If wise men, strangers, travelled dusty roads

to bring rare gifts,

it was for me,

that I might know

that Christ accepts my gifts and welcomes me.

If Mary bore her babe in Bethlehem

at Christmas time,

it was for me,

that I might know

the Saviour of the world who came for me.

The grammar of God

Jesus, Verb of God,

I AM,

now, past, for ever

breaking the bonds of time,

always Mood Active.

Keeping the fire

Snow clouds stripe the moon.

Cold bites, sin stalks, Satan prowls.

Let the fire not die.

The spire

This ancient blade of stone once hewn and raised

to point the way to God and strengthen faith,

affronts the menace of each winter's night,

a geometry to pierce the sky with light

and combat dark without, despair within.

Will there be snowdrops soon to herald spring

and daffodils and birds' deft carolling?

And are there stars beyond the dreary cloud

to guide our glimpse into the infinite?

And is there life beyond the enfolding shroud,

and can we know eternal peace and light?

The spire, sharp spear of faith, outstrips our sight

and points the answer 'Yes'!

Ambition

Strive not for greatness as this world would strive,
for fame which burns a while, then quickly dies,
for passing time erodes such greatness, then
blots every memory from the mind of men.

Seek not for greatness; seek instead to be
My closest friend and walk the road with Me
to holiness of purpose, thought and will,
final perfection thirsting to fulfil.

Pray not for greatness; pray instead to bear
My Spirit's fruit and be My witness here;
accept His seed, prepare a harvest field
which love, joy, peace and every fruit shall yield.

Ask not for greatness; let your heart aspire
to follow Me and servanthood desire,
for he who humbly walks the way I trod
shall be called great before the throne of God.

And this is greatness which shall not decline

nor fade, nor die, though time itself shall cease,

for you shall share the glory that is Mine

and laugh and dance eternally with Me.

Eleanor's spring

This is the first day of spring.

Eleanor laughing runs,

her hair dishevelled in the teasing wind.

She has no purpose to her progress

save to seize

the pure exuberance of life reborn.

Perhaps she is dancing for You, Lord,

and can hear Your pleasure

in the music of the springtime breeze.

Lord, I want to know once more

this pure unbridled thrill of joy in Your grace.

You do not need my endless busyness,

my striving to achieve my petty goals.

You want me, my love, my soul on fire for You,

my life without limits.

Lord, open my cage and let me run for You –

like Eleanor!

For Sakineh

Encircled like an animal at bay

she trembles, weeping and alone; around

the hate-contorted faces scream and mock,

and fists empowered by hate grasp bitter stones.

How should this be? Only a breath ago

she lay contented in her lover's arms

and felt his touch, and let his kisses thrill

and set her body and her soul ablaze...

But there are shouts of anger at the door,

sudden irruption and her lover gone,

betraying her to save his traitorous skin,

while she is roughly clad, and pushed outside

into the street aloud with cries of hate.

There's no escape, no friend; alone she weeps,

disowned by all and shunned; she loved too much.

'Guilty!' they cry as one. 'Root out, expel

the evil from our streets – she shall be stoned!

The Law demands.'

She waits the onslaught, wishing death may come

to assuage the hatred of the circling crowd,

and bring release from dark imaginings

that her soft body he'd seduced in lust

would soon be bloodied pulp, smashed in the dust,

of interest only to the dogs and crows,

object of scorn.

She cowers in dread – and yet no stone is hurled.

Her tormentors are arguing in the crowd

with a young rabbi, stranger to the town.

'Here, you, and tell us what you think! For she

has lived an immoral life; the Law demands

such women should be stoned to rid our town

of all corrupting influence; what do you say?'

The crowd is curious, waiting a response

from this young teacher from the Galilee

who heals and feeds the multitudes and even

(or so it's said) raises the dead to life.

The rabbi utters not a word but stoops and writes

mysterious cryptic letters in the dust.

They throng around Him, pressing loud their case

for justice to be done as Moses said.

At last the rabbi stands; the crowd is hushed

to hear His verdict; shall this woman die?

'If anyone is pure,' He says, 'and never sinned,

then he, and he alone, may throw a stone.'

Once more He stoops, and once again inscribes

His secret wisdom on the thirsty ground,

but none reply. The raucous howls of hate

and clamorous cries for justice fade away.

Her loud accusers one by one retire

and silence reigns.

She waits; is this a dream? Does no one scream

or shout for vengeance and her just deserts?

The rabbi stands. 'Where are they now?' He asks.

'Have none condemned you?' 'No one, Sir,' she sighs.

'Then I will not condemn you; go today

and leave your life of sin – see, you are free!'

She dares to rise; she looks into His eyes,

and in His gaze she sees for the first time

what it means to be loved.

Familiarity

Tonight, Lord, I confess I am afraid.

Your word of life, which only yesterday

spoke to my heart and drew me close to You,

now speaks in muted tones; have I become

so hard of heart?

I read again Your story of the Prodigal,

and in my mind I understood the theme,

but thought that I had read it all before

so many times.

I read, but did not feel discomforted to see

the greed of him who wants his birthright now,

careless if selfish claims pursued inflict

deep wounds of grief.

I read, but did not feel again the bitter pain

of love rejected by a wilful child,

intent on pleasure's selfish wild pursuits

in headlong haste.

I read, but did not feel the haunting fear

that one so loved may not return again,

nor shared the tears which marked that dreaded hour,

their last farewell.

I read, but did not feel the loneliness

of passing days and weeks grown into months,

sad absences from family board and hearth,

and laughter stilled.

I read, but did not feel the pulse of hope
which throbbed and clung unreasonably to life
through dark and lonely nights and empty days,
and would not die.

I read, but did not feel within my soul
that father's love which will not, cannot yield,
but runs to greet and kiss the homeward child,
because he's home!

So Lord, uncloud my eyes, strip bare my soul,
to know my Father's heart which yearns for me,
and let me hear Him singing over me
because I'm home.

The gift of a cross

Which is the gift that shall best celebrate
a love profound, unwavering, such as his?
A present powerful and most eloquent
to speak his longing, show his pure delight
in her, his chosen bride; how shall he choose?
His heart is restless 'til the choice is made.
A cross! Yes, perfect; this is finely worked,
emblem of love which never counts the cost;
fashioned in silver, starred with diamonds too,
clear, clean reflecting sunlight at her breast,
a craftsman's flawless art, matured and honed,
a worthy mark of love; this will he choose.
Would he be jealous if he understood
another lover sought to win her heart
and chose a cross as sign of His love too?
His cross not fashioned by a workman's craft,
in precious gems or silver's polished hue
but blood-stained wood.

For God so loved ... me!

Know, child, that you are loved.
I've loved you since before
the earth's foundations first were laid;
My love for you is sure.

Know, child, that you are loved,
and nothing can us part;
My Spirit ever in you rests,
My presence in your heart.

Know, child, that you are loved;
I send you in My name
to speak My words to those you meet,
My Father love proclaim.

And if the path is dark,
and storms and doubts assail,
even if you cannot see My face
My love will never fail.

Know, child, that you are loved,

unworthy as you feel;

to win your love I gave My Son,

His death your pardon sealed.

Know, child, My child beloved,

you are My joy, My song.

My love for you shall never die

through endless ages long.

Words for the wounded

My child, I love you, always and for ever.

I know your pain,

I have felt your hurt,

I have shared in your suffering,

I have counted your tears as you wept over your failures.

I have forgiven and forgotten the sins which you have confessed before Me; you are pure, holy and welcome in My presence.

Now come to Me and I will give you rest.

I have called you by name and you are Mine.

I delight in you and am proud to be called your Father.

Come to Me and let Me flood you with healing.

Come to Me and let Me say to you, 'Well done'!

Come to Me and let us celebrate our victory – together!

Deep waters

At the margins,

the tall reeds grow, and the ripples of Your grace

fragment the sunlight of Your precious love

into a myriad gems

beyond my counting.

Thus am I rich.

But …

In my unsunned deeps,

carefully screened by the foliage of my fears,

the tangled darkness of my unsubmitted thoughts

hinders the movement

of Your Spirit's life.

Thus am I poor.

Lord, cleanse my all,

and let the water of Your Spirit flow in love

for You alone.

My God, the artist

You are the artist; since You have destroyed

the shroud of death which folds all peoples here

in endless dreary shades of muted grey,

take up Your palette, and apply

the genius of the art You have conceived

for me alone,

unique beloved child.

Thus I may flourish here

and show Your glory to the world

in all the richness of the tints You choose

for me.

Travelling alone

I travel alone

and the world is grey

within and without;

grey clouds,

grey rain,

grey spray,

grey mist-enfolded hills,

grey moisture-laden trees,

grey sheep in dreary fields

enclosed in grey stone walls,

and the grey road streaming endlessly ahead.

Grey in my soul and grey in the skies,

grey, only grey.

The rainbow has been stolen from my world,

hidden from view

within this shroud of drab monotony.

But when I come to You,

You will pour the colours of Your love

into my life.

Living water

Jesus said,

'If anyone is thirsty, let him come,

Let him come to me believing,

Let him drink.'[5]

Jesus, I am thirsty, thirsty for Your holiness,

let me taste Your purity, Your passion and Your power.

Jesus, I am thirsty, thirsty in my emptiness,

let Your presence fill me,

flood me now and thrill me,

let Your Spirit come and refresh me in this hour.

And I will open up my life,

and I will open up my soul.

Living Water, make me whole!

---

[5] John 7:37-38 (author's paraphrase).

Jesus, I am thirsty, thirsty for Your gift of life,

let me feel Your heartbeat, hear the sweetness of Your word.

Jesus, I am thirsty, thirsty in my weariness,

let Your presence fill me,

flood me now and thrill me,

let Your Spirit come to inspire me, precious Lord!

And I will open up my life,

and I will open up my soul.

Living Water, make me whole!

Aberlliedi

Tide rises.

Wavelets fill,

brimmed to overflowing,

every mud-choked channel.

Ripples replicate in every tint

the splendour of the sunset skies,

the artistry of God.

Lord,

send Your grace

to cleanse and fill

my earthbound life,

and let me show Your glory

to Your world.

Wind of God

Immobile in the ocean of my world
I lie becalmed,
entrapped by circumstance and fear.

From north or south or east or west
from anywhere,
I do not care;
just come,
O breath of God.

Breeze, variable, gale or storm
or any other kind
of wind,
I do not mind;
just come,
O breath of God.

I only pray
that You will come and fill my life today,
O breath of God.

Just one word

Just

one

word

changed everything.

My whole life confined within

an unseen wall of silence,

unhearing so unspeaking,

I had thought release would be difficult.

I dared not dream,

I could not know

the power concealed in this young Healer's word.

Ephphatha!

A moment and a single word sufficed

to unstop my ears,

to release my muted tongue,

to teach my soul

wild words of praise of which I'd never dreamed.

Just

one

word.

Are **you** listening?

Encounter

Water into wine.

Amazing!

The wedding feast is over and the guests

are gone contented homeward,

commenting volubly in excited voices

on the beauty of the bride,

the quality of the wine

and the power of the new young rabbi.

Water into wine.

Amazing!

But they are not aware

of the miracle that lies elsewhere,

in me, in us, who served.

He spoke,

and that compelling voice

spoke to us like no other voice

before or since.

We have known, we have heard and seen the truth.

We have met His gaze, we have touched His hand

and drunk His wine,

and we are changed.

Christic in quiet

Within

> A candle flickers in the enfolding gloom
>
> where bread and wine are reverently shared.
>
> The shadow of the cross trembles, recoils,
>
> as if unwilling to recall the memory
>
> of Christ's appalling sacrifice and pain.
>
> Music drifts gently through the quiet air,
>
> eternity in time.
>
> This is the peace of God.

Without

> The sunset whispers to the encroaching night.
>
> Tides swell and fall in ceaseless rhythm while
>
> the toothed rocks and restless surging foam
>
> pursue their struggle for supremacy.
>
> Life is born, life flourishes, then dies,
>
> a transient beauty never replicate
>
> while time shall last.
>
> This is the power of God.

And I, amazed, fall on my knees
to worship Him.

Lee Abbey, September 2012

Communion

My God, the

God of a million galaxies,

God of a billion stars,

reveals Himself to me

in a piece of bread

which I can touch,

which I can taste,

which I can hold

in my hand.

Is this a miracle?

The glory of God

I read Ezekiel, and tried to grasp

the paradox beyond imagining

of ice and fire and vivid rainbow light

and One of radiance incomparable.

For such a vision would I dare to pray?

'Show me Your glory, Lord, I want to see!'

I cried.

And He showed me a man

naked

bloody

beaten

dying on a cross.

Joseph of Arimathea's meditation

A tomb I gave Him,

chill darkness where hope dies, but

to me He gave life.

The cave

You see that cave, that one, that hillside scar,

and heavy stone to keep the entrance fast?

That was a place at my intent prepared

where I shall rest when comes the time for me

to sleep as all my forefathers have slept.

It was for me, you see, and not for Him.

Yet on that day of cruel grief and pain

and many broken dreams and bitter tears

I brought Him here to lie where I should lie.

I thought

this was the least that I could do

for One who made the blind eyes see

and healed the sick and even raised the dead.

And so for Him that cave

became a tomb,

and He was sealed to lie behind the stone,

unyielding stone which robbed the light and wrapped

in endless night the one imprisoned there

where I should lie.

But now the stone is set aside; come see!

He is not there

for He is gone from here I know not where.

The darkness yields, the light becomes reborn.

The tomb in which He lay became

a cave once more,

an empty cave – and suddenly

the world has changed,

for hope has come!

Good Friday

The fatal hammer strikes.

The cruel spike

splinters bone,

tears flesh.

Blood flows.

The man writhes.

Women gasp and turn away.

The sun rises,

birds sing,

flowers bloom,

entirely as usual.

Unreasoned darkness falls.

No birds sing,

no flowers bloom.

This is not usual.

Silent women clutch in fear.

The man hangs lifeless.

This is the death of God.

The Easter joy song

Sing of the joy of that first Easter morning,

graveclothes lie empty, the stone rolled away.

'He is not here!' is the angel's glad tiding.

'See, He is risen,' on this first Easter Day.

Sing of the joy of new hope's sudden dawning;

pain, grief and sorrow had darkened their lives.

The meal is prepared; in the bread once more broken

Jesus revealed; 'Yes, it's true! He's alive!'

Sing of the joy of that first celebration.

'Jesus is living, we've seen Him today!'

Death is defeated, its power crushed for ever;

new hope is ours and our fears swept away.

Share in the joy of each new Easter morning,

Jesus is with us today as our King;

He is alive and He's with us for ever!

Our Lord is here and His victory we sing!

No fixed abode

I live in elsewhere.

Though trammelled strait in time

I grasp eternity.

The Dream

Before the fact there is the Dream,

before the light there is the Dream,

before the word there is the Dream,

before the spring of time is wound there is the Dream.

But now in time the fact is shapen,

but now in time the light is risen,

but now in time the word is spoken,

the Dream gives birth.

The Dream is mine.

The time is now.

God said, 'Let there be light'[6]

And all creation at that voice awoke.

Newbottle sunrise

The sun escapes the shroud

of dreary cloud enfolding distant hills.

Once more that word is spoke:

'Let there be light!'

And God's pure light renewed

pours gold from hilltops to the valley floor,

and lights the dew

on every leaf and stem,

and thrusts the silent rays of day's advance

through the awakening wood

to paint long shadows from each leafless tree

on fallow fields,

and print the image of the oak tree's boughs

upon our ancient lichened rectory wall.

Loud cockerels crow

and sparrows chirp

while by the tussocked tombs

the earliest snowdrops strive to reach the sun.

Come soon, the spring!

The mistral

Today the mistral swept in merciless fury

from his Alpine fortresses,

and rattled the shutters on the old farmhouse

which turned its back and closed its eyes,

having been this way many times before.

We, huddled at our hearthside,

prayed for peace.

Outside

the guardian poplars swayed and whined

and begged for quarter.

Pageant

There is a celebration in the stars tonight.

Beyond the pale light of my window pane

the pageant of the windy skies sweeps past

to go I know not where,

yet from my bed I see

dark islands,

     mountains,

          wondrous animals,

rocks,

     oceans,

        serpents,

          caves and

            fabled birds

parade in unkempt order through the skies,

each silvered by the watching of the moon.

Midnight moon

The winsome moon

larch-cradled rests;

her beauty soothes

and offers healing to

the fractured clouds.

Mandy's tree

Her tree is pretty in pink

(her favourite colour)

blossom this spring.

Her tree

is reaching for light,

yearning for growth,

striving for fruit.

How apt!

Coming of spring

Today

I lay in sunlit peace.

I heard the trees yawn

and watched them stretch their sleep-numbed fingers

to the wakening sky.

Equinox

Fly, grey rainless clouds.

Pale sunlight flees in haste; dark

comes lonely autumn.

Winter at Somerton

Water like glass,

but where the expectant mallards wait

the circled progress of their petty paddling

ripples the mirror of the winter skies.

The boundary between the material and the ephemeral

reflected world

deceives the eye.

The weary sun

retires at last to his hammock of cirrus cloud

strung high between long-shadowed poplars,

and draws across the sky a celestial curtain

of twilight shades

before he sleeps

and yields his kingdom to the encroaching night.

Amazed at such beauty,

appalled at such cruelty,

the world holds its breath.

A love remembered

This bitter winter
oblique rays of setting sun
refuse awhile to die; their dwindling flame
throws haunting shadows on familiar paths.

Now spring's pale sunlight
draws these sere grasses into
resurrection mode; each bloom and bud
betokens love we knew, fresh sprung to birth.

Summer remembers
how woodland shadow sheltered
our innocent meeting; here was spun
the gossamer fabric of our cherished dreams.

Autumn colours flare
then fade; windblown clouds and rain
compel me to my fireside. Here I,
bereft in forest landscape,
ponder our story as the embers fade.

Daneway

This is my place for freedom and reflection.
Curled in a furl of Cotswold's wooded scarp,
this inn of peace offers me gentle welcome,
sun-drenched as cooling cider slakes my thirst.

Yes, I remember Daneway in this summer,
a place and time of cherished memory,
contentment almost perfect in the smile
of God.

But clouds may gather in the summer twilight,
and loneliness still stalks my wounded soul.
Where is my precious friend, God's sweet provision,
beloved companion who should share with me
such times and memories?
Please tell me,
where is she?

Tears

I hate to see you cry your rising fears,

to watch you bowed and shedding pain-filled tears,

the loneliness you've carried through the years

now looming near.

I long to draw you gently to my side,

to hold you in my arms 'til fears subside,

and keep you close until your tears are dried

and peace abides.

I pray to be the light of Christ for you,

to be the earnest of His promise true

that He will stand beside you even through

life's trials too.

This is my content

This is my content –

to lie embraced in your lap

under a clear sky.

A meditation

Lord, it is true, isn't it, that

    truth is stronger than falsehood,

    love is stronger than hate,

    life is stronger than death?

If not, Lord, I could not bear to fall in love again,

knowing that one day it must all come to an end

in tears and grief and pain.

Forgive me, Lord,

I had forgotten how vulnerable are those, like You, who

love.

If You had not broken the circle,

    that absurd futile circle of

        birth

           life

              death

I would live in anxious fretfulness

and never dare to love again.

But You have given me a friend,

and You have given me hope.

Thank You, Lord. You are wonderful to me.

The homecoming

Then I shall rise intent to her warm body,

and we two, though two, become as one.

In seeking each the other's pure delight

in tender touching

    soft caressing

        warm infolding

            hard inthrusting,

as the slow fuse of longings we have shared

at last ignites in flame, we celebrate

the union of the Lover and his Bride.

The womb of the dawn

Your troops will be willing on your day of battle ...
From the womb of the dawn
Your young men will come to you like the dew.
(Psalm 110:3 footnote version)

This is the womb of the dawn,

and in this place of deep and fertile night

primeval living word was first outspoke:

'Let there be light!'

And all creation at that voice awoke.

This is the womb of the dawn,

and here is fusion of the Spirit's might

and love unbounded in the Word revealed.

'I am the Light!'

All darkness vanquished to that light shall yield.

This is the womb of the dawn.

Still it is dark, yet eager to the fight

the young still onward go, banners unfurled.

'You are the light!'

Go, let it blaze, a beacon for the world.

instant ap☐stle

Join the Instant Apostle community!

Visit www.instantapostle.com and sign up for our
newsletter
Follow us on Twitter @instantapostle
Find us on Facebook: Instant Apostle

Check out some of our other great titles!

Potholes and Belly-flops, **Susie Flashman Jarvis**

Susie was a rising star of the modelling world. But she was a private failure, addicted to Class A drugs and promiscuously jumping from one broken relationship to another. Then God...

ISBN 978-0-9559135-8-7

A Book of Sparks, **Shaun Lambert**

Shaun Lambert weaves the ancient disciplines of contemplation with his modern understanding of psychology to unlock a biblical wisdom. Transformation comes through what he calls 'mind*Full*ness', the practice of being filled with the awareness of the presence of God.

ISBN 978-0-9559135-3-2

Less than ordinary? **Nicki Copeland**

Our life experiences, personality and self-opinions shape who we become. This moving story of one woman's struggle with low self-esteem and her journey into self-acceptance will resonate with many, and will inspire and encourage all who are dealing with similar issues.

ISBN 978-1-909728-00-4

A Thorn in My Mind, Cathy Wield

Cathy Wield is uniquely qualified to write on the subject of mental illness as a doctor and a patient. This is her testimony to ongoing healing and maturity while learning to live with serious illness. A must read for those who are affected by mental illness and those who run churches or communities.

ISBN 978-0-9559135-2-5

I'm a Christian – so what do I believe? Ken Gardiner

Ken Gardiner has a passion for Jesus Christ and a passion for truth. Drawing on his rich life experiences of God and his deep biblical knowledge, he invites us to re-examine the essence of the Christian faith.

ISBN 978-0-9559135-9-4

Ernie Gonzales: The Determined Dreamer, Beth Shepherd, illustrated by Lisa Buckridge

Ernie Gonzales is a small, ordinary snail with a big, extraordinary dream! Inspired by his Papa's tales of a legendary snail paradise, Ernie sets out on a daring journey to find it. He is soon swept up in a more exciting adventure than he ever dreamed of.

ISBN 978-0-9559135-7-0

The Tails of Ginger and Tom, Lynne Bradley, illustrated by Susan Briffett

This heart-warming story tells of two energetic kittens, their friend Amber, and her Special Friend, who looks after them all. This is a lovely book for children, and for adults to read to children. Its delightful illustrations will transport you to a world where cats get their paws into everything!

ISBN 978-0-9559135-5-6